THE
GO
Bravely
COMPANION
JOURNAL

THE
GO
Bravely
COMPANION
JOURNAL

BECOMING THE
WOMAN YOU WERE
CREATED TO BE

EMILY WILSON HUSSEM

Ave Maria Press AVE Notre Dame, Indiana

© 2021 by Emily Wilson Hussem

All rights reserved. No part of this book may be used or reproduced in any manner whatsoever, except in the case of reprints in the context of reviews, without written permission from Ave Maria Press®, Inc., P.O. Box 428, Notre Dame, IN 46556, 1-800-282-1865.

Founded in 1865, Ave Maria Press is a ministry of the United States Province of Holy Cross.

www.avemariapress.com

Paperback: ISBN-13 978-1-59471-999-8

Cover and interior images © Katerina Skorik.

Cover and text design by Brianna Dombo.

Printed and bound in the United States of America.

Contents

Introduction

I am so glad you have picked up *Go Bravely* and are embarking on a journey through this book. I poured many hours of prayer and many parts of my heart into it, so I pray that walking through it will be a prayerful experience for your heart! I pray this can be a journey of growth for you as you walk your path of faith with the Lord.

Each chapter in this companion journal reflects the content in the corresponding chapter of *Go Bravely*. At the beginning of each chapter, you will read a testimony quote from a young woman who has read *Go Bravely* and who wanted to share with you why a specific part of the book resonated with her. My hope is that in hearing the voices of other women through these testimonies, you will feel a greater connection to the women whose hearts have been impacted by this book all over the world.

After each testimony is a summary of that chapter, followed by questions and exercises to unpack the chapter's theme and specific points. These exercises are meant to help you look more deeply at the topic and how it relates to your personal faith journey, your heart, and your life. If you need more room for your reflections than the space provided, there are blank pages for journaling in the back of the book. Each chapter is also designed to help you dive deeper into your relationship with God—and for some of you, to strengthen your relationships with the women with whom you are walking through this book! Each chapter ends with a prayer for you to make your own in your conversations with the Lord.

It is likely that the questions and exercises I present in this journal will challenge you—and I have always found challenges to be a good thing because they are what help us to grow! Growth is my hope for you—growth in your relationship with the Lord, in your love for others, and in becoming the magnificent, strong, glorious woman God created you to be.

*In God's name,
let us go on bravely.*

—ST. JOAN OF ARC

ONE

Go Bravely

Hearing about your experiences having to be brave just to open the door for Mass and go in really struck a chord with me! I always thought I was doing something wrong or not strong enough in my faith because I still get scared to live it out, and I've found I need many brave moments to get through. This chapter helped me realize I'm not alone, and also helped me realize that God isn't looking for anything big, but my best effort and asking for his grace in difficult and even scary moments! —Michelle

*Be on your guard,
stand firm in the faith,
be courageous, be strong.*

—1 CORINTHIANS 16:13

Bravery is choosing to do the right thing, even in the face of adversity. Living a courageously countercultural life of faith can be very difficult in a culture that so heavily encourages us to just "go with the flow." It is hard to step out, to look different, to forge a different path, but as women of faith, we live with confidence that it is worth it to do so—that we can choose bravery because we do not live for ourselves, or for the approval of others, but for the greater glory of God. The simple prayer "Jesus, help me to be brave" was a pillar of strength for me in college, and it is a prayer I have used throughout my life in many trials I have faced in living bravely.

It has also been important for me to remember that bravery is often not a feeling. As you navigate the journey of being a woman of faith, a feeling of bravery may come and go—that is where the *choice* to be brave comes in. Choosing to be brave and feeling brave are two different things, and so often in the face of difficulty, that intentional choice to live courageously is the key. It is the choice to do the right thing, even though that choice may make you or others uncomfortable, even though it may cause you to lose people you thought were your friends, even though your heart may be trembling as you move forward in courage!

Go forward bravely, knowing that God is with you every step of the way. He never leaves or forsakes us, and when we call on his name in that simple prayer, "Jesus, help me to be brave," he will help us to make the choice to do so!

TAKE ACTION AND REFLECT

1. Recall a time when you had the opportunity to do the right thing or do what God was asking of you, and you chose not to. What kept you from doing the right thing? Was it fear? Was it fear of what others would say or think? What would you go back and tell yourself in that moment?

2. Have you been inspired by the bravery of a woman or man you know? Who is a role model for you when it comes to living a life of bravery, of doing the right thing in the face of adversity, of living a life of faith that is bold and courageous? Why? Write a letter to this person thanking them for their example to you of what it looks like to go bravely.

3. Recall a time when you made a brave decision. Perhaps you

- wrote a pro-life paper for an assignment and presented it to your class,
- told your friends about your experience on a retreat,
- invited a friend to church or to your youth group,
- ended a relationship that was leading you away from your faith, or
- prayed with a friend in a moment when she needed it.

What helped you to bravely choose to take that action?

. . . .

PRAYER

Jesus, it is not easy to bravely live my faith in a world that discourages me from doing so. It is difficult to swim against the current and to forge a different path than the one chosen by the people around me. When I feel discouraged, please bolster my heart. When I feel afraid, give me the courage to push forward in faith and confidence. When I encounter an opportunity to live bravely and believe that I can't, help me to remember that I can do all things through you who strengthen me. You are my strength, my shield, my fortress, and my guide. Thank you for creating me for a life of bravery. Amen.

You gain strength, courage, and confidence by every experience in which you really stop to look fear in the face. You must do the thing which you think you cannot do.

—ELEANOR ROOSEVELT

TWO

Remember Who You Are

Before reading this book, I was hurt by titles that others were trying to give me. I didn't know who I was, and I thought Jesus had abandoned me. But when I read this chapter, I was speechless. Emily helped me to realize that I am, above all, a daughter of God. No matter what happens to me, Jesus stands with me and loves me. It changes everything. I often try to remember that phrase: "Daughters of God are not weak— they are strong, they are brave, and they shine." —Eleonore

See what love the Father has bestowed on us that we may be called the children of God.

—1 JOHN 3:1

It is easy to believe the lies that our culture, our peers, and many different sources in our lives have spoken to us as young women. I have believed many of these statements I have heard over time: *You are defined by what you look like. You are defined by the number of followers you have. You are defined by your grades. You are defined by your awards and achievements. You are defined by your relationship status.* And if those things aren't impressive or better than other people's, we are simply *not good enough.* These lies we are told bog us down to a point of deep unhappiness, to a point where many women ask themselves, "Will I ever be enough?"

We place our identity in many different things, but these things are only facets of our lives, not *who we are.* As 1 John 3:1 reminds us, the reality is that we are defined by our identity as children of God. This is who we are. We *are* enough because we are God's. But in the midst of a noisy culture that encourages us to place our identity everywhere other than Christ, we must actively and consciously endeavor to derive our worth and our value from our belonging in him each day of our lives.

The good news is that you are a daughter of God—and the good news beyond that is that in Christ you have perfect belonging. You belong to him—that is who you are. That will always be who you are. We, as women, strive to feel as if we belong in many different places, whether that is in our family, in our schools, or in our workplaces, but we must always remember that in Christ, there is no need to strive to belong. You do not have to look, talk, or act a certain way; you only have to exist. There will always be belonging for you in Christ, and this is a truth you can rest in for all the days of your life.

Let us place our identity and worth in Jesus, knowing that in him we are enough, and in him we have everything.

. . . .

TAKE ACTION AND REFLECT

1. Take some time to write out all the titles you hold in your life, accomplishments you've achieved, or awards you've won. It is good to be happy and proud of your hard work, but it is also important to ask yourself if you are placing your identity or finding your worth as a person in one or more of them. Does your self-esteem come from how well you do in that specific area of your life?

2. What, to you, is our culture's view of what it means to be a "normal" woman your age? According to that view, what kind of activities does a "normal" person your age participate in?

3. In what ways does your identity as daughter of God call you to live differently than this "normal" in your current season of life? What are some choices you are making that look different than the choices of some of your peers because you are choosing to follow the Lord with your whole heart?

4. What are some of the hardest aspects of following Jesus for you? What are some of the most beautiful fruits in your life of following Jesus?

5. Do you believe that you have to earn God's love? Take some time to sit with the scripture story of Jesus with the woman at the well (Jn 4:1–42). This is the longest conversation Jesus has in scripture and a beautiful example of his love freely given. The Samaritan woman does nothing to earn Jesus' love, yet he meets her with tremendous love and compassion.

. . . .

PRAYER

Jesus, in the mist of the chaos of voices, it is so easy to forget that I am not any of the titles I hold; I am simply this: yours. Cultivate a deep awareness in my heart that I am made in your holy image and likeness, and that there is nothing I must do to earn your love. Thank you for loving me just as I am and for calling me onward to holiness—for calling me onward to become more like you. I want to rest in the peace of knowing that I am your daughter and, in doing so, help other women to remember who they are and do the very same. Amen.

Before I formed you in the womb, I knew you, before you were born, I dedicated you, a prophet to the nations I appointed you.

—JEREMIAH 1:5

THREE

Be Kind to Other Women

This chapter really opened my eyes to how to handle comparison with grace. Once the horrible feelings of comparison start to creep in, I now remind myself to see every other woman as the beautiful daughter of Christ she is! "If God had wanted me to have the same gifts and talents she has, he would have given them to me. I am called to celebrate who she is and who she was created to be." This quote from the chapter stuck with me more than anything. God created each woman on earth so carefully, and he never repeated a work of art. This chapter has really helped me change the way I think and speak about other women. —Christina

Beloved, let us love one another,
because love is of God;
everyone who loves is begotten
by God and knows God.

—1 JOHN 4:7

It is the natural desire of a parent that their children would get along—and even further, that they would love one another. And the heart of a parent truly breaks when their children do not get along or make the effort to love one another. In the same way, God, our Father, desires that as sisters in Christ we women would support, encourage, and walk with one another in our journey through life. He desires not only that we get along but also that we make the conscious effort to love other women, even when it is difficult.

Womanhood, for many, has come to be a competition where women strive to get ahead, look better, or accumulate more success and achievements than other women. God's design for womanhood was never meant to be this way. The Lord didn't create us to strive to be better than other women; he created us to grow in holiness, become the best version of ourselves we can be, and celebrate our sisters in Christ along the way. He wants us to champion one another as he champions us.

When we rewire our thinking to remember that womanhood is not a competition but a celebration, our outlook can change drastically. When we intentionally root out our own insecurities to find our security in the God who created us, we are more inclined to lift other women up rather than tear them down. This new attitude manifests in our words and actions. Let us endeavor to make those actions and words ones that glorify God and uplift other women in all things. Let us work together to eliminate a spirit of jealousy among women and instead instill a spirit of celebration, support, encouragement, and joy. Let us do the very thing scripture invites us to do—*love one another.*

. . . .

TAKE ACTION AND REFLECT

1. Take some prayerful time to imagine a world where every woman felt free to rest in her brilliant individuality and stunning, unique design. What would that world look like?

2. Have you ever had the thought that every woman around you is more beautiful, more talented, more interesting than you are? What made you think that?

3. Can you recall a moment or season in your life when you started to view womanhood as a competition or other women as competitors in a race against you? How is God calling you to change your perspective from competition to celebration of others?

4. Sit with the word "insecurity" in prayer. Take some time to write about the areas in your life where you feel insecure, either constantly or on occasion. Once you have written them down, hand over each of those insecurities to the Lord with a prayer such as, "God, I place this insecurity in your hands and ask that you transform it into acceptance of myself and confidence in who you created me to be." Tell the Lord about each insecurity, and ask him to touch that area of your heart and life. Boldly ask for deep healing for each of these areas.

. . . .

PRAYER

Jesus, I want to be a woman who brings kindness and charity to the world. I want to be a woman who supports, who
uplifts, and who celebrates the women around me. Please
help me to overcome my insecurities with the help of your
love and healing so I can be that kind of woman. Help me to
see and believe that womanhood is not a competition, but a
journey—one in which I am called to love my sisters in Christ
with the same love you have for them. Cultivate a belief deep
within me that I am beautiful, talented, and amazing because I
am made in the image and likeness of you, the almighty God,
who makes no mistakes, who makes only beautiful things,
and whose plan for each life is good. Amen.

Say to the Lord,
"My refuge and fortress,
my God, in whom I trust."

—PSALM 91:2

FOUR

Depend on Him

This chapter impacted me because it reminded me that I'm on the perfect timeline, just where God wants me to be. I've thought for so many years that in order to be completely happy, at rest, and free, I had to control every aspect of my life and live according to my own timeline, but boy was I wrong. I've learned to let go of trying to control my life by fully surrendering, depending, and having total trust in the Lord, finally finding true happiness, rest, and freedom in him. —Rebecca

*The human heart
plans the way, but
the Lord directs
the steps.*

—PROVERBS 16:9

We are encouraged from all different directions to be "Miss Independent." If we need help from others, we are sometimes made to feel weak or incapable—we have been told that we should be able to "do it all." But as women of faith, we can rest in the truth that Christianity calls us to depend not on ourselves but on God in every part of our lives. We are called to relinquish the attitude of Miss Independent and instead say to the Lord, "Help me to depend on you in all things!"

To depend on the Lord means to surrender to his timing for our lives, trusting that we are never "behind." To depend on the Lord means to commit our work to him, remembering that we can do all things for his glory. To depend on the Lord means to let go of the plans we have for ourselves, knowing that his plans for our lives are far greater than our own. There are many ways we can depend on God, but it must be an intentional action.

If you, like me, have a desire to be in control of things, dependence on the Lord is a daily choice to surrender and to say, "Jesus, I trust in you." This choice begins first thing in the morning, and we can then offer each moment of our day to God and call on his name in moments of both joy and uncertainty or struggle. When the day goes haywire, we can say, "Jesus, I trust in you." When the day is so beautiful that we don't want it to end, we can still say, "Jesus, I trust in you!" To depend on the Lord is to step into the truth of the scripture "We know that all things work for good for those who love God, who are called according to his purpose" (Rom 8:28).

Let us be followers of Christ willing to relinquish control, to step into trust, and to believe that God is our good and loving guide whom we can depend on each day of our lives.

. . . .

TAKE ACTION AND REFLECT

1. Do you have a timeline in your heart, hopes for an overall structure of a plan for your life? Write it out and offer it to the Lord. Hand over your timeline to him in surrender, and say a heartfelt prayer that he would help you trust that his timing and his plan are better than yours.

2. Do you tend to be always looking forward to the next thing, racing ahead of yourself and not experiencing the present?

3. One of the greatest struggles I see among women is the feeling of being "behind" other women in the timeline for their lives. The beauty of our unique lives is that the Lord has a different plan for each one of us. Has there ever been a time when you have felt as if you are behind in life?

4. One of my favorite prayers is one of surrender that my
    husband and I pray together every night: "Jesus, I sur-
    render all of myself to you. Take care of everything." Take
    some time to reflect on this prayer and what it can mean
    for your life and your faith in God.

. . . .

PRAYER

Jesus, you hold all time in your hands. I desire to commit my
way to you and trust in you in all things. When I am tempted toward control, help me learn to surrender. When I am
tempted to despair that my timeline is not coming to fruition,
remind me that your timing is perfect in all things. I trust you;
help me to trust you more. I love you; give me a hunger to
love you more deeply. Amen.

Those whose hearts are enlarged by confidence in God run swiftly on the path of perfection. They not only run, they fly; because, having placed all their hope in the Lord, they are no longer weak as they once were. They become strong with the strength of God, which is given to all who put their trust in him.

—ST. ALPHONSUS LIGUORI

FIVE

Date with Purpose

This is a chapter I've come back to several times. I didn't date in high school, and at the time, I didn't see the point. In the back of my mind, I had the question of "Why?" I felt that none of the boys I knew in high school were willing to lead me to virtue, so I knew I had no good reason to date them, and the lure of popularity or fitting in was not enough to make me want to do so. When I went to college, I came across Go Bravely and read this chapter. I had a couple of dates here and there, but every time I asked myself why I would continue dating that person, I didn't have a great reason. It was only when I met my boyfriend that I knew I had a great reason why I should pursue a relationship with him. Here was a man who led me to virtue warmly and unapologetically, a man outspoken in his faith who pursued me intentionally! Soon I began to ask myself, "Why wouldn't I date him?" All in all, have your "Why?" It is the greatest question you can ask yourself in making the decision to date, or continue dating, someone! —Ana

*Then the peace of God
that surpasses all understanding
will guard your hearts
and minds in Christ Jesus.*

—PHILIPPIANS 4:7

Dating is no easy task in modern culture. With the ever-worsening breakdown of real, honest communication, with a rise in the fear of commitment, in a culture that values ease over effort—dating can be a very challenging thing. As a girl in high school, I was never asked on a date, even though I thought that since "everyone" was dating, I should be dating, too. It was only in retrospect, after I graduated from high school, that I realized that although I may have wanted to date or have a boyfriend, I was not ready to date at all.

When we enter into the world of dating, we should have concrete reasons as to why we are choosing to do so. Dating is not something to approach with carelessness or nonchalance, or something we should do because "everybody's doing it." We should approach it with purpose and intentionality. Evaluating our motives for dating makes the dating process more fruitful—it gives it purpose. And ultimately, the purpose of dating someone is to see if you are called to marry each other. Now, that's not something you must figure out on the first date, or even six months in, but it is important to be clear that this is the *purpose* of dating. Being clear about the purpose of our actions is a gateway for peace . . . and dating should be a peaceful process!

Dating is not an essential part of a particular season of life, and it is not something you should ever feel pressured to do but, through prayer and maturity, an action you freely decide to take. Putting pressure on *anyone* to date is not a mature or respectful thing to do—choosing to date is a decision you make when you feel comfortable to do so. There is no rush, and no matter what anyone says, there will never be any rush!

Another important thing to remember is that women who date a lot are no more spectacular than women who do not. You do not become wonderful when a guy tells you that you are—you are, and always will be, a wonderful work of the almighty God, fashioned in his image and likeness. If a guy notices that about you, terrific! If a guy does not, it does not take away from the reality of who you are. Do not ever forget this.

. . . .

TAKE ACTION AND REFLECT

1. For single girls: Do you feel pressure from any outside factors to date—whether that's from your friends, from your family, or because everyone else seems to be doing so?

2. For girls in relationships: Take some time to think about the purpose of your dating relationship. Why are you in this relationship? Is it making you a better person? Is the boy you are dating leading you to Jesus? Answer these questions honestly to help you dig deeper into your reason for dating.

3. As a Christian woman, I have found that surrender is key to the entire concept of dating. Surrender of our desire to date, or where we'd like a relationship to go, or our desire for one specific guy to notice us . . . when we surrender these desires freely to the Lord, great peace can enter our hearts as we trust in God's will for our lives. Take time in prayer to think honestly about your heart's desires regarding dating, and offer them over to God.

. . . .

PRAYER

Lord, help me to approach dating with purpose and clarity in my heart and in my mind. Whether I am single or in a relationship, help me to honestly answer the question of "Why?" Reveal the motives of my heart to me, and please walk with me and give me the courage to make good decisions in this area of my life. Help me to see with clear eyes and a clear heart and to walk closely with you as I keep my heart hidden in you. Amen.

When a man loves a woman, he has to become worthy of her. The higher her virtue, the more noble her character, the more devoted she is to truth, justice, goodness, the more a man has to aspire to be worthy of her. The history of civilization could actually be written in terms of the level of its women.

—VEN. FULTON SHEEN

SIX

Just Keep Swimming

My favorite chapter was "Just Keep Swimming." I can be brutally harsh with myself in ways that I would never be with others. I have always dwelled on times when I made the wrong choices. Regret, guilt, and obsession are each familiar to me. With more serious mistakes, I can hold on for years. In "Just Keep Swimming," Emily wrote that failing does not make one a failure, and that mistakes are a normal facet of what it means to be human. —Bridget

*The one who sat on the throne said,
"Behold, I make all things new."*

—REVELATION 21:5

It can be embarrassing to fail. Making mistakes or choosing to sin (especially when it hurts other people) can be difficult to move on from when we feel deeply regretful, embarrassed, or even ashamed. At times in my life, I have dwelled on regrets to the point of losing sleep and crying about them years later. Over time, I have found that this is not the way Christ wants us to live!

Dwelling on our past mistakes is like driving a car while constantly looking in the rearview mirror at what is behind us. Can you imagine how dangerous that would be, never looking ahead at what is in front of you? It is the same in our lives! Our lives are not meant to be spent looking in the rearview mirror at all of our past mistakes and failures. We do need to look back every so often on events or choices from the past in order to learn, to grow, to change, and to heal. But we were not created to wallow in our regrets to the point of exhaustion and depression. We are to live looking forward and believing in the mercy of God—and choosing to show mercy to ourselves when we make mistakes.

We are invited to believe and trust in the forgiveness God extends to us and to extend that forgiveness to ourselves. When we stall out in self-criticism, focus on our failures, or struggle to move past our mistakes, the Lord invites us to live in the present and to look forward to what is in store. We follow a God who declares that he can make *all things new*. If we believe in this, and trust in this, there is no reason to dwell in regret—but reason to rejoice and keep swimming.

TAKE ACTION AND REFLECT

1. Are there failures in your life or mistakes you have made that you struggle to let go of and move past?

2. Find a quiet time to pray with the Lord. Imagine yourself sitting with Christ in the midst of the mistake or failure you tend to dwell on the most . . . maybe it was a friendship you ruined, a bad decision you made, something you said or didn't say in one specific moment. Now, picture Christ with you in the midst of the mess, in the depths of your disappointment with yourself, speaking these words of truth to you: *"Behold, I make all things new."* Then imagine him lifting you up to move on.

3. When I begin to dwell on past regrets, I have found it helpful to quietly say the word "forward" to myself. This stops my thoughts before they spiral into even deeper regret. If this is something you struggle with too, try using that word to interrupt any dwelling on the past and to reframe your vision to look forward.

PRAYER

Jesus, help me to remember that I am a human who will make mistakes, that I am an imperfect person who will fall and fall again. Help me, in all aspects of my life, to know that life is a learning process and that I will continually have opportunities to take action from what I have learned. Free me from the belief that I have to be perfect, that I must get everything right the first time, or that I am a failure because I have failed at something. Help me to grow in the virtue of humility, that I may face my mistakes and failures with a heart willing to rise and begin again. Amen.

Let no one mourn that he has fallen again and again; for forgiveness has risen from the grave.

—ST. JOHN CHRYSOSTOM

SEVEN

Find Your Gaggle

Growing up, I didn't have that "best friends group." I had friends, but our relationships felt as if they were just surface level. I always desired real and authentic sisterhood like Mary and Elizabeth . . . friends who rush to your side in a time of need, friends who see Christ in you, friends you can be completely yourself with. My desire for this type of friendship just grew stronger as I went through high school, but I still didn't find it, so I asked God to give me the grace to be faithful to him because I knew he would be faithful to me. And sure enough, he was! I just had to trust the path God was leading me on, which was leaving my hometown for a nine-month mission trip. The friendships I formed with my team were exactly what I prayed for, real and authentic. I truly believe this is what God was preparing my heart for in high school, because he showed me the gold in these friendships. My advice is to be faithful to God and the gold he has in store for you. Community looks different for everyone. —Emily

Faithful friends are a sturdy shelter; whoever finds one finds a treasure.

—SIRACH 6:14

It is no secret that cultivating authentic friendship with other women can be very challenging. Authentic friendship does not just happen; it takes investment, care, forgiveness, and dedication. Friendship is also difficult because we bring our wounds and sensitivities into each relationship. These can slow us down in growing closer to other women and in overcoming obstacles in friendship when they arise.

For followers of Jesus, finding friends can be even more challenging! The majority of young people do not practice any faith at all, so finding women who passionately share our beliefs can sometimes be like searching for a needle in a haystack. Not every friend must have the exact same values we do, but every friend must support and not discourage us from living out the values that are most important to us. In true, lasting friendships, our friends lead us to what is right, stand by us in good times and in hard times, and encourage us to become the woman God created us to be. These closest friends on our journey should share the same goal—the goal of spending eternal life in heaven with God the Father, Son, and Holy Spirit.

It is also important for us to evaluate the kind of friend we are to others. Are you the kind of friend you want others to be for you? Sometimes we may complain about our fair-weather friends, who are present when times are good and absent when they are not, but if we are honest, we might need to admit that we tend to do the very same thing to our friends. Are you, like the geese I describe in this chapter, providing uplift for your friends and leading them to Christ?

This must always be our goal—to lead our friends ultimately to Jesus. He is the way, the truth, and the life, and leading our friends to him is the greatest gift one friend could possibly give another.

. . . .

TAKE ACTION AND REFLECT

1. Think about the friends in your life you are grateful for (maybe that is one or two close friends, or maybe more come to mind), and pray for each of them by name. Thank God for the specific aspects of that person that you appreciate, and thank him for the times that person has accompanied you when you were in need. Pray for that person and for any area in their life that you know they need prayers for.

2. Write a letter to someone whose friendship means a lot to you. Tell them why you are grateful for them, how they have reflected the light of Christ to you, and anything else you would like them to know.

3. Not all friendships are meant to last forever—friendships may end for a multitude of reasons. Sometimes friends choose different lifestyles, they may move away from one another and drift apart, or one person in the relationship may realize that their friend is not leading them to virtue and that it is time to end the friendship. Take some time in prayer to evaluate the friendships in your life. Who do you call your friends, and do they deserve that title? Are there friendships you know you need to move away from?

4. What kind of friend are you? What are your strengths as a friend, and in what areas do you need to improve?

. . . .

PRAYER

Jesus, what a gift it is to have friends to support me in this journey through life. Thank you for each friend I have had along my journey so far, and for the friends I have today. Give me strength to be a good friend, to be a good listener, to be a woman who leads my friends to what is right. Help me to be a woman who leads my friends to you. Amen.

But Ruth said,
"Do not press me to go back
and abandon you!
Wherever you go I will go,
wherever you lodge
I will lodge. Your people
shall be my people
and your God, my God.
Where you die I will die,
and there be buried.
May the Lord do thus
to me, and more,
if even death
separates me
from you!"

—RUTH 1:16–17

EIGHT

Choose Chastity

My favorite chapter was "Choose Chastity." I really am trying to take that chapter to heart. I already am saving sex for marriage, and I actively profess that fact proudly with friends and on social media (I don't care what other people think about that); it's more about what I consume daily from the media (mainly TV shows and YouTube). Sometimes I become a bit too complacent (if that's the right word) about what I watch. I don't watch anything super explicit, but sometimes I don't realize how what I am watching isn't furthering my journey of chastity and purity, or I do realize it but I don't stop watching it. —Gretchen

*Every man is the builder
of a temple called his body.*

—HENRY DAVID THOREAU

Often when people hear the word "chastity," they think of saving sex for marriage, or simply choosing to abstain from sex. The beauty of the virtue of chastity is that it encompasses so much more than the decisions we make with our physical bodies—it also includes the decisions we make in regard to our minds, hearts, and souls. Chastity involves living out our sexuality in the healthy and wholesome way God designed it, which is not an easy thing to do in our sex-saturated culture.

Chastity is a complex, beautiful virtue we are called to strive for if we profess ourselves as followers of Jesus. One of the first ways we can progress in chastity is to evaluate what we are consuming with our eyes, ears, and hearts. We must take inventory of the shows and movies we watch, the music we listen to, and the social media accounts we follow to make sure they are leading us toward purity of heart, not away from it—leading us to Christ, and not away from him.

Another, more obvious way we live the virtue of chastity is by honoring God with our bodies and in our relationships. This is challenging in a world that sees sex as nothing more than a physical sensation. In a hookup culture, striving to live purely is entirely countercultural—but the truth that we know as daughters of God is that the choice to live chastely will set us free. As followers of Christ, we are commanded to choose the road of purity in romantic relationships—to honor the body of the man you are dating and to make certain that he honors your body as well.

When a woman chooses the countercultural road of living chastely, she will never wonder if her boyfriend is with her for the right reasons. She can focus on developing other interests and pastimes with the man she loves. On this road, she is free from the worry, fear, regret, and sorrow that can come with allowing herself to be used by a man who has promised nothing to her. On this road, she can dwell in peace with a mind and heart filled with beauty and goodness rather than the filth and vulgarity so prominent in our culture. With this choice, she can walk the road of authentic love, honoring and respecting herself and others.

. . . .

TAKE ACTION AND REFLECT

1. When you hear the word "chastity," what comes to mind for you?

2. Have you ever been made fun of for choosing to live
    chastely, whether that's a choice to save sex for marriage,
    not go with your friends to an inappropriate movie, or
    something else? How did that make you feel?

3. What are some activities you can take part in with your
    significant other that will help you two have fun together
    in chaste ways?

. . . .

PRAYER

Lord, I ask for a greater understanding of the virtue of chastity and the way you want me to pursue it in my life. Enlighten me to see the beauty of living chastely, of choosing purity for my mind, my heart, my body, and my soul. Free me from any misconceptions I have about chastity, and reveal to me the value of this virtue and its importance in my life. Give me a greater desire to fill my life with truth, goodness, and beauty, and the courage to show the people around me the freedom that comes with living this virtue. Amen.

Blessed are the clean of heart, for they will see God.

—MATTHEW 5:8

NINE

Be Open to the Jump

My favorite chapter was "Be Open to the Jump." I accepted an amazing job in Switzerland and moved here for two years after I changed the "What if?" question to "Why not?" —Henriett

Life with Christ is a wonderful adventure.

—ST. JOHN PAUL II

Taking risks can be difficult. It is much easier to do what I am comfortable with, to live inside the familiar. What I have found as a young adult woman, however, is that staying within total familiarity does not stretch me or force me to grow. It does not help me to cultivate virtue or become a better woman. Remaining inside my comfort zone allows me to stay exactly as I am, prompting these questions: Do I want to develop as a person? Do I want to grow? Am I willing to experience things that are perhaps uncomfortable or unfamiliar so that I can learn more and become more fully the woman God created me to be?

The answer for me, and I hope for you, is "Yes!" We want to spend our lives growing and becoming the women God created us to be, but that means we must challenge ourselves. We must not always take the comfortable, easy route. We must not remain stagnant. We must take risks and step outside of our comfort zones to learn or experience something fantastic and new.

Those risks will look different for every one of us. Some of us may sign up for an eight-day silent retreat when we have never been on a silent retreat before. Others may join a local outreach program to the homeless. Others may take courage and stand up and give a speech in front of their class or school. Risks come in all forms, big and small, but all are uniquely challenging in their own way—and each one gives us the opportunity to grow, change, and draw closer to Jesus in positive and beautiful ways.

TAKE ACTION AND REFLECT

1. What is something you've always wanted to try but have never mustered the courage or made the effort to do?

2. Think about a time when you took a risk and were glad you chose to do so. Write about it. What was scary about that risk, and what helped you overcome your hesitation or even fear to take that risk?

3. Do you, like me, fall frequently into the mindset of "What if?" Of thinking about all the things that could go wrong? Where in your life can you change your mindset from "What if?" to "Why not?"

· ·

PRAYER

Dear Lord, I want to change and grow throughout my life, but it can be scary to take the risks necessary for that growth. Help me enter into a spirit of "Why not?" when I am presented with opportunities that will help me become more fully alive. Even in the midst of fear, help me to take leaps of faith that will allow me to trust more fully in you and the abundant, courageous life you have called me to live. Amen.

To have courage for
whatever comes in life—
everything lies in that.

—ST. TERESA OF AVILA

TEN

Honor Those Who Love You Most

A part of this chapter that resonates with me is when Emily writes that there are different ways we can honor our parents. For me, my dad has hurt me emotionally in the past few years. I learned in this chapter that by praying for him, I am still honoring him in the way the Lord asks me to. The chapter also discusses how we can honor our parents by having respectful conversations with them, even in times of disagreement. Ultimately, love and respect are two gifts we receive from God that we are called to show our parents, and there are many ways we can express that love and respect to them. —Mikaela

Honor your father and your mother, as the Lord, your God, has commanded you, that you may have a long life and that you may prosper in the land the Lord your God is giving you.

—DEUTERONOMY 5:16

God's simple, yet profound call to honor our parents is so important that he included it in the Ten Commandments! Depending on what our relationships with our parents have looked like over the years, obedience to that command is easier for some of us than for others. However, the act of honoring someone can take many different forms. Some of us may honor our parents in the way we speak to them and interact with them as we navigate living with them at home. Others may honor their parents by caring for them when they cannot care for themselves. Those of us whose parents have passed away may honor them by praying for their souls and living out what they taught us.

It can be easy to complain about our parents to other people. Whether it was a disagreement we had or some habit of theirs that we find frustrating, it is tempting to take the route of airing out our grievances about our parents to others. And so I ask you: What would it look like if, instead of complaining to others, you brought your concerns and grievances to God first?

What if you took your frustrations with your parents to God in prayer and asked for a heart to respond with patience and love? Whatever way God is calling you to honor your father and your mother, he wants to guide you and give you the courage and grace to do so. He wants to give you the courage to honor this commandment because, in doing so, you honor not only your parents but also *him*.

Let us endeavor to love our parents in the way Christ calls us to—with patience, love, compassion, and forgiveness.

TAKE ACTION AND REFLECT

1. Sit with the fourth commandment in prayer. Ask the Lord specifically what that commandment means for you in your life right now. Ask him how he is calling you to live out this commandment in obedience and faith.

2. Reflect on the things that you have learned from your mom that you are really grateful for. Perhaps those things include a virtue, or a way of living, or a recipe. Write those things down.

3. In the same way, reflect on the things that you have learned from your dad that you are really grateful for. Those things may include a hobby, a passion for something, or a virtue. Write those things down.

4. Spend some time in prayer for each of your parents. If you are holding on to any grudges or hurts from them, offer those to God during this time. Ask God specifically for what you need in your relationships with your parents— whether that is patience, love, intentionality, acceptance, gratitude, forgiveness, or some other quality.

. . . .

PRAYER

Lord, I ask you to give me the grace to honor my parents well and, in doing so, to honor you, my God, whom I love above all else. Help me to see the good in my parents, to look for the ways each of them has taught me something beautiful about life. Grant me the grace to speak to them with love and respect, and to speak about them to others with charity. Grant me the grace to forgive them for the ways they have fallen short in their humanity, for the mistakes they have made, for any hurt they have caused me that I still harbor in my heart. Please grant them the grace to forgive me for any hurt I have caused them in return. Amen.

In the twilight
of life, God will
not judge us on
our earthly possessions
and human success, but
rather on how much we
have loved.

—ST. JOHN OF
THE CROSS

ELEVEN

Give It All You've Got

The prayer in this chapter, "God, I offer this work to you. Help me to give you glory in it," is so beautiful. I find myself saying this when I'm wishing I was somewhere else such as at home with a family instead of at work. It helps me focus on where God has me at this moment. St. Mother Teresa said, "Bloom where you are planted," and I try to take this to heart and help the ground I'm in be fertile by giving it all I've got! —Jenny

*Jesus did not say,
"You will never have a rough
passage, you will never be over-
strained, you will never feel
uncomfortable," but he did say,
"You will never be overcome."*

—ST. JULIAN OF NORWICH

Our culture teaches us to work hard so that we can achieve success, money, and prestige. It tells women they will have to work extra hard climbing the corporate ladder to achieve the success they dream of. But as followers of Christ, we know that the goal of our hard work is not money, or fame, or accolades—but to give glory to God.

Every woman who reads this book will be called to different work—and that work will be an avenue by which she can give God glory. My first job as a teenager, dusting glasses in an optical store, may have seemed meaningless and solely a way to earn money, but that work could give glory to God through that simple prayer, "God, I offer this work to you. Help me to give you glory in it!" As I took jobs at pizza places and amusement parks, I wasn't achieving success or earning very much money, but I was doing my best to pray through my work and offer all of it to God. This was not easy to do on busy nights, waiting six tables at once, but I know God sees our efforts even on our worst days at work!

Whatever type of work we do, Christ calls each of us individually to make a positive impact in the world. This is not always a grand thing affecting thousands of people. It may mean positively affecting the lives of twelve elderly people in the nursing home where you volunteer or encouraging the small children in your classroom as you live the ministry of your teaching. Let us each offer ourselves wholeheartedly to the work Christ has called us to do, giving him glory through it.

· ·

TAKE ACTION AND REFLECT

1. What do your daily duties look like at this time in your life? Are you in school, working, or something else? What is required of you to attend or complete each day?

2. What are some ways you can actively offer these daily
    duties to God?

3. Have you thanked God lately for your education or your
    job? We often forget, in the midst of difficult assignments
    or tough days at work, that education and employment
    are valuable gifts that we should not take for granted.
    Write out a prayer of thanksgiving to God for the season
    you find yourself in and for the daily duties by which you
    can give him glory.

. . . .

PRAYER

Jesus, I want to give you glory through all of my efforts. Whether that is in my work, in my hospitality to others, in my efforts to make a positive impact during my life—I want to give it all I've got and praise you in it. Help me to combat laziness and apply myself wholeheartedly to my day's work— whether that is in school, at an office, or waiting tables. May I show others the value of hard work and make every class, every shift, every day an opportunity to give you glory with my life! Amen.

And whatever you do, in word or in deed, do everything in the name of the Lord Jesus, giving thanks to God the Father through him.

—COLOSSIANS 3:17

TWELVE

Love Yourself

After reading this chapter, I realized I have to love myself before I can realize my real worth and value to those around me. Until I can see that I am made wonderfully, I cannot fully experience love. I have to accept my flaws and quirks and see that those are the very things that someone will love about me if I first accept and love them . . . and I absolutely loved the mirror affirmation. —Amanda

*My name is _____ and
I love and accept myself.*

*My name is _____ and
I am a beautiful and radiant
daughter of God.*

Loving yourself can come across as a vain thing to do in our self-obsessed culture. What does it mean to love myself as a woman trying to follow Jesus? It means to learn to love the woman God made me to be. This type of love is vital because if I learn to love myself first, I can then love others well. "Love your neighbor as you love yourself" is a common translation of the Golden Rule. If I treat myself—my heart, my mind, my body—with love and respect, I will be more apt to do the same for others. If I love myself even in my imperfections, mistakes, and failures, I will be more apt to love others in the midst of all those facets of their lives, too!

Sometimes I speak with women who are afraid that if they learn to love themselves, or grow too much in confidence, then they will become conceited or prideful. It is key to remember that confidence does not necessarily mean pride. Confidence can blend with humility when it is rooted in the Lord—in the fact that he made each of us unique, beautiful, and gifted in our own ways. The beauty of every woman, her gifts and talents and the unique light that she brings to the world, all point back to God the Creator. When I live with an awareness that the Lord made me *good* and *beautiful*, I can learn to love the woman he made me to be and give him glory in that confidence. That confidence can pour out into a vibrant love of others. As women, we should constantly pray for confidence and humility, both rooted in the heart of Jesus.

To make the choice to love yourself is a gift you can give yourself, and something the Lord desires for you. You are his handiwork, and he desires that you would love his handiwork. To work on our confidence takes real effort, but it is effort worth making!

. . . .

TAKE ACTION AND REFLECT

1. In *Go Bravely*, I suggest looking at yourself in a mirror and speaking positive words into your own heart. What are three things that come to mind when you stand before a mirror and think about the things you love about yourself? Write them down.

2. Is there a woman in your life who exudes confidence mixed with humility? A woman you feel comfortable with, because she shows what it means to rest in who she is and who God created her to be? Who is that woman, and what about her reveals this to you?

3. Take some time to pray with Psalm 139:13–14: *"You formed my inmost being; you knit me in my mother's womb. I praise you, because I am wonderfully made; wonderful are your works! My very self you know."* Speak that verse out loud a few times in prayer, and see what words stand out to you. Ask Jesus for a deeper belief in the words, *"I am wonderfully made."*

· ·

PRAYER

Lord, it is easy to fall into self-criticism rather than loving the woman I am and accepting myself for who you created me to be. I want to live as a woman who accepts that you made me just as I am—in my appearance, in my intelligence, in my gifts and talents. You knit me carefully together in my mother's womb, and I want to rejoice that you made me unique and unrepeatable. Help me to come to a deeper acceptance of myself, the woman I am and am becoming, so that I can joyfully accept others. Amen.

For we are his handiwork, created in Christ Jesus for the good works that God has prepared in advance, that we should live in them.

—EPHESIANS 2:10

THIRTEEN

Clothe Yourself in Strength

This chapter had a great impact on my outlook of how what I wear reflects who I am as a person. God created me to be his daughter, in his image. God created me as a work of art, a temple, to honor him. The way I dress outwardly reflects and represents who I am as a person. By choosing to wear clothes that honor and respect God, I am helping others to focus on his good work.

Before I read this chapter, I did not understand this. I thought clothes dictated how cool, trendy, or popular you are. I thought that dressing and wearing clothes to honor and respect God meant wearing clothing that hid me. But I learned from this chapter that I can still honor God while wearing cute, feminine clothing. I want my appearance to be a good example to other girls and to show them that you can still be fashionable and respectful! But overall, I choose to buy and wear clothing that represents me while also respecting and honoring God! —Amelia

*Do you not know that
your body is a temple of
the Holy Spirit within you,
whom you have from God, and
that you are not your own?*

—1 CORINTHIANS 6:19

Innumerable times throughout my life—through advertisements, through celebrities, through social media—I have been told a lie, and maybe you have, too: The more skin you show as a woman, the more powerful you are. The more revealing your clothes are, the more comfortable you must be with yourself. It is hard to see past these falsehoods so prevalent in our society. It is hard to see why any woman should bother to try to dress modestly at all.

As a young woman, I heard talks in church and on retreats that were always centered on making choices for my wardrobe based on what would help the young men around me be more virtuous. As I grew older, I reframed this understanding of modesty for myself—that I want to dress with dignity because I am a woman of God, made in his image and likeness with infinite value and worth. This was a very important reframing for me—I decided I was going to choose my clothes to reflect my inherent dignity and to honor God. I realized when I did this that, in turn, I was helping my brothers in Christ strive for purity!

I decided to base my choices of clothing on this question: "Does this outfit reflect that I am a woman of dignity and value, a woman who knows that God dwells within her?" This question has helped me greatly as a Christian woman striving to live virtuously across every facet of my life. Dressing with your inherent value and dignity in mind sets you free to allow your personality, your intelligence, and your authentic feminine strength to shine. It allows you to know that when a guy shows interest in you, he is not showing interest because of revealing clothing—but because he wants to get to know your mind and heart.

TAKE ACTION AND REFLECT

1. What does the word "modesty" mean to you? Does the word bring up any feelings (positive or negative)?

2. Have you, like me, struggled with the reasons you have been given for dressing modestly? How has this chapter given you a different outlook?

3. Take some time in prayer asking the Lord to reveal to your heart what the virtue of modesty truly is. Ask him to strip away any preconceived notions or struggles you may have with the word, and let him speak to your heart about what he is calling you to in living out this virtue. Write about what comes up during this time of prayer.

. . . .

PRAYER

Jesus, I ask that you reveal to me a deeper understanding of the virtue of modesty and its importance in my life as your follower. Help me to see the beauty of my body, the inherent value and worth that will always be within me. Give me the courage to make the countercultural choice to dress modestly, outwardly showing the world that my strength, my worth, and my belonging are in you. Amen.

I am not afraid . . .
I was born to do this.

—ST. JOAN OF ARC

FOURTEEN

Forgive and Forget

This chapter impacted me because forgiveness is something I have always struggled with. When people hurt me, I tend to hold on to that pain and resentment. Around the time I read this chapter, I had been going through a lot of struggles with mental health. Many girls who I thought were my friends seemed to take this as an opportunity to take advantage of my vulnerability, and they spread rumors and treated me poorly. For a while I was hurt and angry. This anger and lack of forgiveness was blocking me from God and from embracing love. This chapter helped me to realize that God calls us to forgive and that forgiveness is one of the most loving things we can do. Holding on to pain and resentment takes up space in our hearts that should otherwise be filled with the mercy and love of God. —Carol

Put on then, as God's chosen ones, holy and beloved, heartfelt compassion, kindness, humility, gentleness, and patience, bearing with one another and forgiving one another, if one has a grievance against another; as the Lord has forgiven you, so must you also do.

—COLOSSIANS 3:12–13

It is easy to convince ourselves that holding on to grudges takes less effort than letting go of them. Choosing to forgive others for serious pain they have caused us requires real effort, effort that doesn't come easily, and often doesn't even come out of our own strength, but the strength of God. But the reality is this—holding on to grudges takes effort, too. You must carry them around like a burdensome bag of bricks, rather than being set free from the weight they are causing your heart and mind.

Jesus Christ models perfect forgiveness, and he also models the reality that forgiveness is a choice. In his time on earth Christ exemplified forgiveness, most notably as he asked God the Father to forgive those who had just nailed him to the Cross:

"Father, forgive them, they know not what they do" (Lk 23:34). As he hung on the Cross waiting to die, Jesus Christ forgave, and he has forgiven you and me for our sin countless times since then. Forgiveness is a choice that Christ wants to strengthen us to make every day of our lives because in forgiveness there is freedom—and Christ created us for a life of freedom.

Choosing to forgive someone does not undo the hurt they caused; it does not even take all of the pain away. But it does propel us into the freedom Christ created us for—the freedom of living as a merciful person, one who forgives others as he forgave us (Mt 6:12). To forgive others is to be Christlike; to show others what it means to forgive is to be the hands and feet of Christ in the world. May we choose the difficult path of forgiveness and, in doing so, show others the freedom found in a life of merciful love.

· ·

TAKE ACTION AND REFLECT

1. Are there people in your life you need to forgive? Who and what situations come to mind?

2. There are times when we need to forgive other people, but there are also times when we need to forgive ourselves. Have you held back from forgiving yourself for something you've done or failed to do?

3. Spend some time in prayer reflecting on the gift of God's mercy freely given to you. When was the last time you thanked God in a heartfelt way for his mercy? When was the last time you stopped to soak in the reality that God did not *have* to forgive our sins but *chose* to forgive out of love for us? Thank God for his mercy, and see what comes up in your heart in your conversation with him.

. . . .

PRAYER

God, I don't want to live my life harboring grudges and holding things against people, carrying around a heavy weight. I
want to live in the freedom of mercy, in the beauty of extend-
ing mercy toward others and accepting mercy for myself.
Please give me the fortitude and humility to be a merciful
and forgiving person. Teach me how to forgive others just
as you extended forgiveness to those who nailed you to the
Cross. Help me, by my example of mercy and love, to reflect
your love into the hearts of those who have hurt me. Amen.

*Forgiveness is above all
a personal choice, a decision
of the heart to go against the
natural instinct to pay back
evil with evil.*

—ST. JOHN PAUL II

FIFTEEN

Keep Calm and Follow God

Discerning my vocation in life has always been a source of anxiety for me. How do I know if I'm following God's will? How do I determine the difference between God's plan for my life vs. my own? In this chapter, Emily says, "Before we talk about marriage, single life, or consecrated life, we must recognize that the first and overarching call of our lives is to be the hands and feet of Jesus Christ in the world." After reflecting on this, I established a better prayer life and personal relationship with the Lord. It was soon after that my anxieties for the future subsided. This chapter also taught me that my vocation is not just some blurry picture in the future, but a daily testimony of my own gifts and talents. With a fuller trust in God, I know he has a great plan for my life, and I am open to listen to wherever he leads me! —Devin

I am the good shepherd, and I know mine and mine know me.

—JOHN 10:14

Throughout my journey of faith, I have too often fallen into the belief that following God's will for my life is like trying to get through a maze, blindly attempting to figure out which way God wants me to go next or what decision he wants me to make. This has led to many stressed-out seasons of prayer, thinking God is being secretive and sly rather than leading me faithfully and clearly as a good shepherd leads his sheep. This was certainly true of my quest to discern the vocation God was calling me to as a Catholic woman—whether it was a call to marriage, to the religious life, or to the single life.

The image and reality of Jesus as the shepherd can be very transformative in faith. When it comes to discerning our vocation, the Lord isn't driving us in fear or anguish, and we don't have to figure it out all by ourselves; instead, as our shepherd, he accompanies us on our life journey, and beyond that, he is present and guiding us every step of the way. He guides us in love and compassion. His will is not something to grasp tirelessly for, but something to ask him to lead us to. He did not tell me, "You are called to marriage; go figure it out!" In his goodness, he led me to my husband, and through much prayer and discernment, I felt called to the vocation of marriage.

The most important thing to remember in discerning our vocation (or discerning anything at all in our lives!) is that God's voice is one of peace. He leads in peace. He guides in peace.

When I think of a shepherd, I think of gentleness—letting his sheep out to pasture and patiently guiding them along the way. That is who Christ wants to be for each of us in discernment of vocation. With his rod and his staff (Ps 23:4), he wants to comfort us and guide us as we respond with courage, fortitude, and joy.

TAKE ACTION AND REFLECT

1. Do you fear that the Lord will take something from you if you open yourself fully to him? What are you afraid of him taking away? Talk about that with him.

2. Take time in prayer to reflect on the scripture of the Good Shepherd (Jn 10:14–18). What about this scripture passage stands out to you?

3. Do you feel stressed about the "need" to figure out your vocation? Do you feel pressure to solve the mystery as soon as possible? Where does that pressure come from?

4. Read through the final quote in this chapter slowly, a few
    times. What parts of it stand out to you? What fears do
    you have about where the Lord is leading you in your
    vocation?

. . . .

PRAYER

God, thank you for always leading me with love. You are a
gentle and loving shepherd, and for that, I give you praise!
I ask that you cultivate deep belief within me that you lead
me in love and do not ever drive me in fear. Help me learn to
recognize your voice as I follow you, the voice of my Good
Shepherd, and give me the courage to say yes to your call as
you lead me forward in my life. I believe and trust that there
is nothing to fear when you are at my side—that you only call
me, your beloved daughter, to things that are for my good
and for your glory. I want to follow you. Amen.

Cast yourself into
the arms of God
and be very sure
that if he wants
anything of you,
he will fit you for
the work and give
you strength.

—ST. PHILIP NERI

SIXTEEN

Exercise Your "No" Muscle

This chapter really hit home because I am a person who is always trying to be everything for everyone, even at the expense of my own health. This chapter really helped me realize that it's okay to say no to people or things so that I can prioritize, so I can get what needs to be done done and also have time for myself, so that I can make sure I'm taking care of myself mentally, physically, and spiritually. Saying no is definitely still a struggle for me, but this specific chapter got the ball rolling on learning how to do this. It taught me that I don't always have to be putting everyone else before me, and that there are times it's okay to put myself first. —Heather

*Now the Lord is the Spirit,
and where the Spirit of
the Lord is, there is freedom.*

—2 CORINTHIANS 3:17

Children are experts at use of the word "no." As their wills begin to develop in their toddler years, they realize that there are some things they just do not want to do, and they make sure that the person in charge knows it! Strong-willed children can be a huge challenge for parents, but as women of faith trying to stick to our values in a world lacking in virtue, we can learn something from them.

We must, in a way, resurrect our attachment to the word "no." We must, day by day, learn to say no to the things that will lead us away from the Lord and yes to the things that will lead us to him. It's certainly not easy, but as a young woman of faith I came to see that every time I said no to sinful choices or patterns of behavior, every time I said no to the temptations of the evil one, every time I said no to following the crowd rather than forging my own path of faith, I was saying yes to a life of freedom and joy.

To learn to say no took practice. It was like building muscles in the gym; you must do bicep curls again and again in order to get defined muscles, one curl at a time. In the same way, every time I said no to something that would not lead me to Christ, it got a little bit easier to say it the next time. And saying no when I needed to built up my strength and resolve to follow the Lord.

Sometimes we follow the crowd and say yes to things we don't want to do or that we know are not good for us because we don't want people to be upset with us. It is essential to remember that pleasing God is far more important than pleasing others, and that *we* are the ones who must take care of our own hearts. The word "no" can seem like a negative thing, but in a life of faith, learning to say it is a positive step on the path of following Christ with fortitude, courage, and perseverance.

TAKE ACTION AND REFLECT

1. Recall a time that you wanted to say no but did not. Why didn't you say no?

2. Recall a time when you said no and were so glad you did. What helped you to make that choice? Why were you glad you said no?

3. Have you ever been made fun of for saying no or doing things differently? Write about how that made you feel.

4. Are you a people pleaser? Do you often feel tempted to say yes to things you may not wish to do (such as going to parties, sending sexual photos to guys, keeping secrets for your friends, gossiping or making fun of others) just because of what other people will think?

. . . .

PRAYER

Jesus, help me to see that in a life lived following you, the word "no" has power to help me live a life of freedom. Give me the courage to use the word "no" when I know it is necessary. Give me the strength and resolve to be concerned with pleasing you through my actions, words, and deeds rather than those around me. Help me to believe and trust that every no to sin is a step that leads me closer to you and your heart, which is the very place I want to be. Amen.

Our life, in order to be Christian, has to be a continual renunciation, a continual sacrifice. But this is not difficult, if one thinks what these few years passed in suffering are, compared with eternal happiness where joy will have no measure or end, and where we shall have unimaginable peace.

—BL. PIER GIORGIO FRASSATI

SEVENTEEN

Love Your Body

This chapter really stood out to me in a particular way. It spoke so much truth into my heart, knowing that the Father created me exactly as I am. Exercising doesn't need to be a punishment. It is a choice to glorify the Lord with my body.
—Matalie

Take care of your body with steadfast fidelity. The soul must see through these eyes alone, and if they are dim, the whole world is clouded.

—JOHANN WOLFGANG VON GOETHE

With the overwhelming number of airbrushed and doctored images we see on a daily basis, it can be difficult to love the bodies God gave us. Do you ever see images flash across social media and think, *If only I could look like that, then I would finally be happy with myself?* I have had this thought many times. It's hard to ignore the seeming perfection in outward appearance of the many women who appear on our screens every day through social media, television, and advertising.

But when I have that thought, I must then stop to ask, *Is it really looking like someone else that would make me happy? What is keeping me from accepting the body God gave me, and drawing happiness from that acceptance instead?* That thought changes my entire perspective.

Our bodies reflect both our cultural heritage and the uniqueness of our DNA. And instead of doing everything we can to try to fit the mold that we think is perfection, God wants us to take care of our bodies, be kind to them, and accept their differences. When we exercise and when we eat in a healthy way, we are taking good care of our bodies. In this way we can honor the God who created us—the God who made each of us, mind, body, and spirit, in his image and likeness.

Choosing to love our bodies is a lifelong decision; our bodies change over time as we age and perhaps bear children. God invites us to a consistent choice to take good care of ourselves and to praise him that we are wonderfully made each and every day. He truly desires this for us. He wants us to be confident women, because when we live in confidence in who he created us to be, we can step into the freedom he created us for.

TAKE ACTION AND REFLECT

1. Write down three things you love about the body God gave you. These may be physical attributes, but they can also be skills or abilities.

2. Do you struggle to love your body? What are some of the highs and lows you have experienced in your journey to accept the body God created specifically for you?

3. Go for a walk today and pay attention to the movements of your body as a time of purposeful prayer. Give thanks to God during the walk for every part of your body, from your heart to your feet to your circulatory system, praising him for crafting you so carefully and thoughtfully!

· ·

PRAYER

Lord, I am thankful that in the scope of all that you have thought to create in this world, you thought to create me. Thank you for my body that you so carefully crafted in my mother's womb. Thank you for my breath, for my life, and for all the abilities of my body. Help me to love and celebrate your handiwork manifested in me. Help me to take good care of the body you have given me. Help me to make positive choices for my well-being so that I can be as happy, healthy, and strong as you created me to be. Amen.

I praise you, because I am wonderfully made; wonderful are your works! My very self you know.

—PSALM 139:14

EIGHTEEN

Ignore the Haters

I loved this chapter because it really hit home for me. I grew up getting bullied for all different things, what I looked like, and how I acted. As Emily shares, when you hear these things over and over, you start to believe they're true. I made the decision that if people were not going to like me for who I was, I was going to have to get them to like me for something I wasn't. I started letting my "friends" make all the choices in my life, who we spent time with, what I dressed like, what I talked about, and I was so unhappy. I knew I wasn't satisfied, but I was so afraid that if I spoke out for myself, I would be alone, that all the lies I grew up being told by my "friends" would end up being true. A line that really struck me is at the end of the chapter where Emily says, "He delights in who you are and created you to take part in his divine plan for the world." It helped me realize that I am so much more than the lies that the world tells me. I am a beautiful daughter of God, and no bully can take that away from me. —Analisa

All the darkness in the world cannot extinguish the light of a single candle.

—ST. FRANCIS OF ASSISI

Rejection can be deeply painful—betrayal even more so. Betrayal by friends is a lonely and difficult road to navigate. And when we face this road, it is key to remember that Jesus walked it before us. Jesus was betrayed by his own friend, Judas Iscariot, in the days before his death (Lk 22:47–48), and even Peter, who had spent so much time with Jesus, denied knowing him three times (Mt 26:34)!

If you have faced rejection or betrayal by friends, it can be easy to internalize the pain this caused you and let it affect you for many years to come. That is what I did for a very long time after experiencing rejection by the people I thought were my friends in college. I had to fight against the lie they had spoken to me—that nobody wanted me to be around—and realize that although they may not have wanted to be friends with me, that was not true for everyone. I had to choose to believe that even though these so-called friends did not love me, I was still lovable, and there were people in the world willing to accept me for who I am. Not only that, but I had to choose to believe that I would find people who could be trusted in friendship—people who would not talk behind my back, people I could lean on when I was vulnerable, people with whom I could share in the mutual giving that happens in friendship.

And so, as I let God heal me of the words that were spoken to me, I invite you to pray for healing of the areas where betrayal or persecution have harmed you or hardened your heart. May God bring restoration and healing to the hearts deeply affected by the hurtful words or actions of others. The Lord wants you to believe the truth that you are not a burden—that there are people who truly do enjoy your company, who love you for who you are, and who genuinely want you around.

. . . .

TAKE ACTION AND REFLECT

1. Have you had an experience of being rejected? Write about that experience and how it made you feel at the time.

2. It has been helpful for me to imagine myself as I walked
    back from that hurtful conversation with my friend in
    college (crying my eyes out!) to imagine Christ walking
    alongside me, weeping with me for how I felt. Allow your-
    self to go back to the moment where you faced hurt from
    the rejection of others, and picture Jesus there with you.
    Imagine the comfort you feel in seeing his presence in
    that moment. What does he say to you?

3. Have you held on to a lie that was spoken to you about who you are? Perhaps it is that you are not intelligent, that nobody likes you, that you are ugly, that you are unlovable. Take some time to imagine yourself sitting with Jesus, and imagine him speaking the exact opposite of that lie to you. Perhaps you hear him say . . . *You are loved. You are beautiful. You are accepted. You are lovable. You are good enough. You are smart. You are strong.* Make a heartfelt prayer that the Lord would erase the lie that was spoken to you with the truth that he speaks in that moment.

. . . .

PRAYER

Jesus, it has been difficult to be hurt and betrayed in my life. I am grateful for your compassion because you know exactly how it feels to be hurt by someone you love. Please help me to remember the truth you speak about who I am. Give me the confidence to know that I am not a burden and that there are people in my life who enjoy my company and want to support me in being me. Help me to remember that there are trustworthy people in this world, people who are open-hearted, loving, and good. May I be one of those people to each person you place in my path. Amen.

I am loved, worthy, and set apart for God's great purpose for my life. He delights in who I am and created me to take part in his divine plan for the world. I am not a burden. There are people who enjoy my company, who love me for who I am, and who

genuinely want me around.
I will not let what anyone
else says or thinks ever convince
me otherwise.

. . . .

Blessed are you when they
insult you and persecute you
and utter every kind of
evil against you (falsely)
because of me.
Rejoice and be glad, for your
reward will be great in heaven.

—MATTHEW 5:11–12

NINETEEN

Radiate with Light

"Radiate with Light" was so helpful in debunking the lie that because I don't have a St. Augustine conversion story, my story cannot be impactful. It helped me come to a deeper awareness that the Lord longs to use the joys and struggles of my life to draw others to himself and that I need to cooperate with him and be willing to boldly share the Gospel. It was such a pragmatic guide for learning how to evangelize simply and authentically. —Larisa

Sharing your testimony reflects the light of Christ directly into the life of the person you are sharing with.

It is a common misconception that someone's testimony is only compelling if it's filled with dramatic twists and turns, if it's a story of falling far away from Jesus and then returning home in repentance like the prodigal son. My own testimony is not very dramatic at all . . . while I haven't led a perfect life, I have always tried to stay close to Jesus, have always gone to church, and have always done my best to make faith a priority in my life. And if your testimony is like mine, it matters just as much as the testimonies of people like my friend Andrew, who lived a life of parties and drug use before having a deep and radical encounter with Jesus and choosing to follow him.

Every story of faith matters because every story of faith points back to Jesus himself. Every testimony matters because it reflects the unique way that God calls each of us to his heart. And each of us is called to share our story of faith with others. This can be a daunting task, as it is not a popular thing to be a woman of faith—you may be made fun of or mocked for living your faith openly. The good news is that many souls have gone before us who were not afraid to share the great things God has done. Just think of St. Peter and St. Paul and how impactful their witness has been for thousands of years to this day!

The first step toward radiating with light is to reflect deeply on your faith journey, every part of it from the beginning until today. When were you introduced to Christ? Have there been twists and turns? Who has accompanied you well on your journey? In a faith journey, every point on the map matters—nothing was happenstance; no point along the way was missed by the Lord. He has been present for every part of it and desires that you would share about your journey with courage and with faith.

. . . .

TAKE ACTION AND REFLECT

1. Set aside some time to write out your testimony in your journal. Whether it has been filled with twists and turns or you've been on a steady path throughout your life, write about your faith journey.

2. Prayerfully consider what your answers would be if someone asked you today, "Do you believe in God?" "Why should I believe in God, too?" or "Why do you go to church?"

3. Have you ever allowed fear to be an obstacle to sharing your faith with someone?

4. Take some time in prayer to reflect on the scripture about the light under the bushel basket (Mt 5). Imagine that you are holding one candle that is lit, representing your faith. Imagine that when you share your faith with someone else, it lights the candle they are holding. Imagine that this person passes the light on to another person, and so on. Sit with the imagery of how impactful sharing your light with one soul can be, how it can impact many souls beyond that one.

. . . .

PRAYER

Lord, I do not want to hide my light in fear of what others may say or think. I want to boldly tell of your love, of the great sacrifice you made for each soul when you gave your life on the Cross. Give me the courage to share my testimony freely and to evangelize with love. Help me to learn more about how I can share my faith with others and tell the world about you. I want to be a witness. I want to shine the light you've given me and bring you glory. Amen.

You are the light of
the world. A city set
on a mountain cannot
be hidden. Nor do they light
a lamp and then put it under
a bushel basket;
it is set on a lampstand,
where it gives light
to all in the house.

—MATTHEW 5:14–15

TWENTY

Live It Up

When I was a kid, I thought that being a true Christian meant praying all day and not enjoying life . . . this idea wasn't really attractive to me. I also thought that saints were sad people who were only suffering, so I was a little bit scared of being a Catholic Christian. As life went on, I met some people who were full of joy, radiant, enjoying their lives, and, what's more, they loved Jesus. And guess what? Suddenly Christianity was really attractive. When I was reading Go Bravely I was on holiday, and I remember the moment when I was reading the chapter "Live It Up." I immediately started to enjoy the sea, the taste of my ice cream, singing birds, the hot summer breeze . . . I felt so happy and thankful to God. I enjoy a tasty meal, morning sunshine, great books, the smell of flowers, chats with friends, family evenings with board games . . . because while I am enjoying all of these, I am praising the Creator of all goodness and joy in this world. —Nina

The soul of the one who serves God always swims in joy, always keeps holiday, and is always in the mood for singing.

—ST. JOHN OF THE CROSS

Through my conversations with women over the years, I have come to realize how often we fall into the notion that if you are a woman who loves God, you cannot enjoy your life. You cannot be happy, because God doesn't want you to be happy. You must spend every second of your life in prayer and heavy contemplation. How untrue this notion is!

God did not create us for a life of sorrow. Is suffering a part of life that Christ allows for our good and for his glory? Certainly. Did God create us just for the purpose of being happy and having fun? Certainly not! Life has its share of difficulties and happiness, and we are called to give God glory in it all. And in the midst of the difficulties of life, joy can be a great witness to others of the beauty faith brings to our lives. Joy is an attractive quality—people are drawn to it. On the other hand, people are turned off by negativity and those who cannot seem to find the good in anything. Joy is a powerful witness to the beauty and magnificence of a life lived with Jesus.

Jesus is the light of the world. And he wants you to live in this light and share that light with others. You can share that light on your soccer team, when you are out to dinner with friends, in your career, or even on a summer day spent on the lake. When we recognize that every good and perfect gift is from above (Jas 1:17), we can enjoy the beauty of every facet of our life and give thanks to the God who gifted us with it. Living with a spirit of gratitude can change our entire life. Every day is a gift not to be taken for granted, and God desires that we would delight in this magnificent life we have been given.

TAKE ACTION AND REFLECT

1. What are some of the things you really enjoy? Maybe a special hobby, laughing with a friend, a delicious meal, traveling, watching the sunrise, hiking or camping, cooking with your grandma? There are thousands of facets of this earthly life to appreciate and enjoy. Think about those and reflect on them as gifts given specifically to you by God.

2. A spirit of gratitude is very important in the life of a Christian. Do you intentionally practice gratitude in your everyday life? Set aside some time each day for a week to write down a few things you are grateful for. See how it changes your perspective!

3. What are some of your most joyful memories? Perhaps they include a specific family vacation, a graduation, a memorable birthday party, or even just one spectacular summer day with your friends that you will never forget. Write about those memories and the joy you felt as you experienced those moments, and thank God for them!

PRAYER

Lord, thank you for creating me for a life of joy. I want to rejoice in the life you have given me and be a cheerful witness to your love in this world. Give me the grace to remember that my faith is not a bag of bricks to be carried around, but a reason and cause for joy. May I never stop sharing the light you've given me—in song, laughter, enjoyment of friends and family, dancing, creativity, through every good and beautiful thing you have created.

May the God of hope fill you with all joy and peace in believing, so that you may abound in hope by the power of the holy Spirit.

—ROMANS 15:13

Journaling Pages

EMILY WILSON HUSSEM is an international speaker, author, and YouTuber who runs a global ministry for women. With more than 120,000 subscribers on YouTube and 67,000 on Instagram, she reaches a worldwide audience of women with a message of faith and identity in Jesus.

The author of the bestselling and award-winning *Go Bravely*, *Awaken My Heart*, and *I Choose the Sky*, she earned a bachelor's degree in broadcast journalism from Arizona State University. Wilson Hussem lives in Southern California with her husband, Daniël, and their children.

http://emilywilsonministries
Facebook: @emilywilsonministries
Twitter, Instagram: @emwilss
Youtube: youtube.com/emilyywilsonn

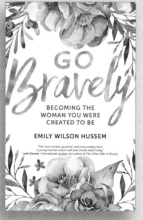
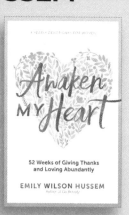